KJV
Old Text
New Poetry

KJV
Old Text
New Poetry

edited by
Joan Norlev Taylor,
Adrian May
and Pam Job

Wivenbooks 2011

Cover illustration:

1639 Edition of the King James Bible courtesy of the Albert Sloman Library, Essex University.

Design: Catherine Dodds

ISBN 978-0-9557313-8-9

www.wivenhoebooks.co.uk

Since childhood, the rhythm and powerful simplicity of the language of the King James Version have haunted my imagination. They laid down an indelible bedrock of word and image so evocative and profound that, for me, no modern translation can touch it. The Psalms, the Song of Songs, the strangely accurate mystery of the Gospels (Christ pierced in the side, the sponge soaked in vinegar and raised on a reed) simply sang along the vein. This is what poetry was all about.

Pauline Stainer

CONTENTS

PREFACE

It is like a grain of mustard seed, which, when it is sown in the earth, is less than all the seeds that be in the earth:
But when it is sown, it groweth up, and becometh greater than all herbs, and shooteth out great branches; so that the fowls of the air may lodge under the shadow of it.

Gospel of Mark 5: 31-32

The genesis of this anthology came, somewhat Biblically, in a sudden flash. As a historian of religion, at King's College London, I was surrounded by news about the 400th anniversary of the King James Version, the rich and resonant English language edition of the Bible first published in 1611 under the auspices of King James I of England and Wales (King James VI of Scotland). I noted in my email inbox nearly every week that there were events celebrating the anniversary, and updates on a forthcoming conference based at King's College London, to take place in July 2011. As a creative writer, this started to resonate.

I had for some time been using the Bible as a resource for my own poems, particularly drawing on the KJV, even though as a scholar I knew it to be based occasionally on incorrect manuscripts of Greek and Hebrew, with its English language sometimes too archaic to be easily comprehensible. But I love the KJV as I love Shakespeare, and the Bible I seem to have always had, with beautiful illustrations by E. S. Hardy, is the one embedded in that layer of my mind where poetry forms. At Christmas I wrote another poem with the sound of this text hovering in that layer, echoed through nativity plays and cards, and then it dawned on me that this process could be the foundation of a collective project, and a celebration.

I ran it past three friends, three of course being one of those Biblical numbers. Firstly, I talked to Adrian May, lecturer in creative writing at Essex University, whose energetic poetry collection, *An Essex Attitude* (Wivenbooks, 2009), had been followed by a work for students, *Myth and Creative Writing: the Self-Renewing Song* (Longmans, 2010), with its picture of Innocence by William Blake on the cover. I discussed it with Pam Job, poet and secretary of the organising team of *poetry*wivenhoe, a community-based poetry initiative that brings the UK's most interesting poets to read in the arts-friendly environment of Wivenhoe, the little town I like to call the cultural capital of the Colne Estuary. And then I took the idea to Ginny Waters, bookshop entrepreneur and publisher of Wivenbooks. All three were keen to make this project happen: an anthology of work from those poets we hoped would accept the challenge to reflect on the KJV in some way, in any way they liked. In the 400th anniversary year of the KJV we then asked some of our favourite new and established poets to contribute to a collection that uses this great work of English literature as a resource for their creativity.

Thus it was born: a collaboration of three friends inviting, editing and publishing this collection. We aimed to have the book ready in six months, and we have succeeded thanks to the great generosity and enthusiasm of our contributing poets, who threw themselves into the task with admirable care. We have been astonished at the supreme quality of the work we have received, on time, by those we have solicited.

What do we think of the KJV now? The KJV comes from a past age, when it drew out the meanings of texts from another past, long ago. Now we approach it variously. For some the Bible is sacred text. For others the KJV is not so much the message of God's interaction with humanity but rather an outstanding work of English literature. Whatever way you use it, this robust text is not to be ignored.

Our anthology therefore celebrates the KJV, and also celebrates the art of poetry. The collection is generally arranged in order of the books of the KJV, with the relevant Biblical text preceding the new poetry.

Proceeds from the book will go to *poetry*wivenhoe, to use towards giving more contemporary poets the chance to read their work (and sell their books). Yes, we are just doing this for love, singing the praises of a book of old and the activity of poetic inspiration. We want to share this with as many poetry-loving people as possible.

Call it a mustard seed.

Joan Norlev Taylor

FOREWORD

*poetry*wivenhoe, the beneficiary of this anthology, was established in Wivenhoe four years ago when a group of local poets met to discuss the viability of running a monthly live poetry event in the town. Every month from then on *poetry*wivenhoe has brought some of Britain's most interesting up-and-coming and established poets to Wivenhoe to engage with a vibrant poetry-hungry audience. We have built up a networking operation with a peculiar dynamism; poets recommend us to others and ask to bring their new collections. *Poetry*wivenhoe pay them a fee and their travel costs, so the more we can raise with this anthology, the more poets can benefit from the opportunity to share their work.

This not only supports the poets, but also the local community of writers. We wanted to offer our audience the best in contemporary poetry by inviting nationally known poets to read their work and also to encourage the development of poetry writing in the community by having an 'open mic' session where local poets can read.

The venture has proved a great success and, partly because the standard of poetry read at 'open mic' was so high, and also to further stimulate interest, we inaugurated the Wivenhoe Poetry Competition in 2009. Resulting from that, a successful and exciting anthology, '*poetry*wivenhoe', was produced and another volume will soon be on the way. The competition thrives.

For myself, having moved to Wivenhoe from London seven years ago – another Biblical number of course – I had no idea that this would be the beginning of a whole new chapter in my life, one where poetry would take centre stage. I joined various writing groups, set up a poetry reading group with a friend and, of course, became involved in *poetry*wivenhoe which has been an invaluable stimulus and resource for us all.

As for my relationship with the KJV, it has to be a personal one, given my surname – first recorded in the fourteenth century in Norwich, and possibly the name given to someone who played the Biblical character Job in the medieval mystery plays. No other version of the Bible captures the quality of poetry in the Book of Job and offers the subtlety of the range of emotions it expresses. For me, KJV rules and always will and it is a continuing source of inspiration: it is comforting to think, as a poet, that out of our mouths 'go burning lamps, and sparks of fire leap out.' (Job 41: 19).

Pam Job

INTRODUCTION

UNAUTHORISED VERSE

Although it is possible for a poet, or any other kind of writer, to relate to a book in a conventional way, poets deal with the exceptional and their relationships to other texts are therefore likely also to be exceptional. This is probably particularly true of a relationship with the Bible. It might even be the troubled, therefore exceptional, seemingly conventional, relationships of others to it which makes the Bible appealing to the poet. The appeal is not just something clever, and especially, I think, not even religious in any normal way.

My own relationship with the Bible starts, in my mind, with a mystery suitable to the ancient craft of poetry, in a kind of ritual passing on of the potential of arcane knowledge by a mentor. I was led into a labyrinthine second-hand bookshop by a fellow poet, well versed in the mysteries. I'd admitted that I didn't have a useable copy of my own. All I had was my Mum's miniature Bible, which was in too delicate a state of repair to handle much. He found me a decent, standard sized KJV by Collins for a couple of pounds. It's the one I still use frequently, with the weight of its potential as a gift of occult inspiration. The sense of being able to find hidden depth in the old text, made unfamiliar by its very familiarity, made cool by its least likely to be thought so associations, was something I sought from fellow writers: a way of finding the exceptional in the apparently common, or forbidden by fashion, place. The Bible was so unlikely, it became far out.

The way a poet might think about the Bible is then one that embraces its tendency, both in content and reputation, to call to the taboo, in the sense of its special as well as forbidden qualities. Like a myth, the Bible offers up and responds to the core of trouble it addresses and commands. This is miles away from the fundamentalist rationalism or literalistic narrowness which public debates tend to focus around.

So we turn to the Bible for what's surprising about the stuff we thought we knew, just as the poet looks at life for its hidden quality, for its revelation. Reading the poems in this book might then be comforting or offer some certainty, but they are just as likely to do the opposite, which is as it should be. This book is in the mysterious shadow of the other, or the Other, I could say, so is a kind of reverence, even if it is an unauthorised one.

What it might make happen is that you wander to a boot sale, jumble or charity shop and, having checked for the introduction about people being resistant to new versions, to make sure it is a KJV, wander through its strange tales in wonder, marvelling at your rebellious compliance, your irreverent reverence, your familiarity with the old language's unfamiliar, self-renewing appeal. This book might be your mentor. These poems might make you ready.

The old stuff is weird, not corny. The old order and authority is compelling and challenging, not merely oppressive, though it can be that too – but so can Facebook. The exciting way that people who are not conventionally religious want to connect with their own beautiful, English mystery language source-book this year is itself inspiring.

Let the debates about translation, authenticity, historical fact, interpretation and scholarship go on. Poets might rather turn us on to the troubled, the mysterious, the wondrous, the crucial potential of this most 'suggestful' of books, which itself sings though our culture untamed, as it does in our own responses, our own unauthorised verse.

Adrian May

THANKS AND ACKNOWLEDGMENTS

We would like to thank Ginny Waters for taking on this project as part of the enterprises of Wivenbooks, and also the other members of the *poetry*wivenhoe organising team, for their support and enthusiasm, particularly Mike Harwood. Thank you especially to Catherine Dodds, whose cover artwork is perfect, and for her brilliant ideas and labours to get it that way. Thank you to Faith Ressmeyer for the donation. Very many thanks also to Nigel Cochrane, Deputy Librarian at the Albert Sloman Library of the University of Essex, for material for the cover image, scanned from the library's 1639 edition of the King James Bible.

We thank the following for permission to reprint previously published work: Peterloo Poets, for Christine Webb's three poems, all of which come from her collection *After Babel* (2004) and Enitharmon Press for 'let us' and '& when he came to it', from Mario Petrucci's *i tulips* (2010) and for 'In Latter Days' from Kevin Crossley-Holland's *The Language of Yes* (1996). Robert Vas Dias' 'The Secret Starer' is part of the sequence, 'Speak to Me Silently: Still Life and Poetry' from his book *Still · Life and Other Poems of Art and Artifice* (2010), thank you to Shearsman for this. Katrina Naomi's poem 'Jacket' first appeared online in www.likestarlings.com and subsequently in *goldfish 3*, Goldsmith's anthology of new writing (London, 2010) and Anne Ryland's poem 'Rebekah' was first published by *Chapman* 110 (January 2010). We are grateful to both for permissions granted.

Most of the work in this collection is published here for the first time.

The Translator

(In memory of my ancestor Robert Tighe, d.1616)

I

Anne Browne's grandfather, he turned out to be.
No wonder she bequeathed books in her will:
'*Charnocks sermons upon the attributes
and Doctor Burnetts church history*' – these
to a son-in-law; then '*Item I give
to my daughter Hurst my Cambridge Bible*'.

That Bible might have been a clue; first, though,
where was she from: Kirby? Careby? Some small
Danelaw village near the Rutland border
in Lincolnshire. They all sounded the same
to the vicar of St Mary Woolnoth
in London when he married her parents.

But two years later, 1631,
in the register at Carlby, '*Anne Tigh
daughter to John Tigh baptised June vij*'.
John was swallowed up in the Civil War;
during which same commotion Anne married
Samuel Browne of Stockinghall, Rutland.

Carlby, then. But the register patchy,
no earlier Tighe entries, John's mother
buried as her second husband's widow
'Marie Bawtrie' (to be unmasked later).
So who was her first? The Lay Subsidy
returns, for the land tax, surrendered him:

in the 8th regnal year of James I,
'[...] Tyghe doctor in Divinity' – first name
obliterated. It doesn't matter;

there was only going to be one match.
The Oxford and Cambridge alumni lists
rolled out his multiple identities:

'Tighe, Robert, of Deeping, Lincs. BA from
Trinity College, Cambridge. BD and
DD, Magdalen College, Oxford. Vicar
of All Hallows' (from whose tower Pepys would
view the fire). *'Archdeacon of Middlesex.*
One of the translators of the Bible.'

II

Being him:
sifting through flakes and flecks
of Hebrew; winnowing out
seeds of meaning; choking
on obscurities, the chaff
of mistranscriptions, howlers,
ambiguities, the never-before-seen.

Dreaming it:
the braids of upside-down-looking
words trailing through his sleep,
tripping him up or winding themselves
into suddenly obvious patterns:
truth leaping out;
no room for argument.

But arguing anyway:
someone, Tyndale or whoever,
may have got it wrong –
just this one term,
perhaps, for a beast or a tree;
an odd verb; a tribal name;
a turn of phrase that needed to be recast.

III

After all, they had chosen him for it:
celeberrimus textuarius –
the lad from a dull yeoman family
in Deeping St James, who went to Cambridge
and grew into a 'profound linguist'
(as Fuller has it) – rose to his moment.

After his doctorate, after he left
scholastic seclusion to get an heir,
found a wife and a parish, began to
baptise his own children (most of whom died),
and stuffed the graveyard with plague burials
while the new Scottish King quaked and delayed,

came the call: to join the First Westminster
Company under Lancelot Andrewes
and re-examine an allotted chunk
of the Old Testament. Andrewes himself
took the Pentateuch, with a few yes-men;
Tighe and his fellows broached the histories.

Elsewhere, companies of learned divines
combed their way through the Hebrew and Greek texts
of the remaining Scriptures (without pay –
their other duties had to support them)
for some five years: conferring, reviewing,
meeting again, squabbling for perfection.

Selden relates how they went about it:
one reading, the others interrupting
to correct any fault. It was all done
by voice, testing it on the ear for sense
and euphony. Almost no one took notes.
The great process lies buried in hearsay.

IV

And Robert? No sooner excavated
from the silt of documentary darkness
than he slithers away again: a black gown
among other such around a table,
offering suggestions when the urge impels him
but not, it seems, writing anything down.

We have his signature as vicar
on page after page of the register
at All Hallows; but otherwise
no identifiable word of his:
no letters, no books or sermons,
even his will declared invalid and lost.

He has merged into a composite –
we can make contact with that mind
only in his assent, grudged or willing,
quite often tacit, no doubt,
as the procedural rules enjoined,
to Joshua, Judges, Ruth, Samuel, the books of Kings.

Fleur Adcock

And the LORD God formed man *of* the dust of the ground, and breathed into his nostrils the breath of life; and man became a living soul.

And the LORD God planted a garden eastward in Eden; and there he put the man whom he had formed.

And the LORD God took the man, and put him into the garden of Eden to dress it and to keep it.

Genesis 2: 7-8, 15

let us

talk
lip to lip as
though morning

just made us –
parted these
mouths

wan
as clay to
make way for

words that are
for us to
try

first
time on air
deft as dew on its

leaf – so let me
speak as an
adam

might
whose moment
is under a kind god

who looks on a half-
made garden
& come

eve
-ning will
change his mind

Mario Petrucci

Genesis I–III: Four Jottings:
(Void, Man, Woman, Snake)

1

And the earth was without form, and void; and
darkness *was* upon the face of the deep.
Genesis 1: 2

O harder storm than woman clung lifelong.
O unimaginable wordlessness.
Black water, black the wind, and no birds.
Flung back to bear it, how the eyeball reels
unsocketed and pours its seeing out
in chasms dark as needles, gales nail-sharp.
Can a will wind among these wild winds?
A god speak to such bleak and sodden void?

2

And the LORD God formed man *of* the dust of the ground.
Genesis 2: 7a

Nothing could be as sudden as this garden.
One mist of rain and instantly an orchard.
From absolutely virgin soil, abrupt,
two trees rise above honeysuckle, roses,
two prohibitions, meant for whom? But look
a dredge of dust, thumb-patterned in a trice,
suddenly strolls as lightly as a camel
under the branches of his destiny.

3

And the LORD God caused a deep sleep to fall upon
Adam, and he slept: and he took one of his ribs, and
closed up the flesh instead thereof.
Genesis 2:21

Pishon of Havilah, a land of gold,
Gíhon of Kush, the rivers Híddekel
and great Euphrates – set the boy amid them,
anaesthetise and gash the flesh just formed,
rip ribs, fold blood, to mould a glimmering girl.
So the one's element is grit of the road,
the other's – brittle bone. And now surround them,
these innocents, with risk, temptation, threat.

4

And the serpent said unto the woman, Ye shall not
surely die.
Genesis 3: 4

Of course, of course, of course you shall not die!
Snatch the ripe fruit. Whoever made the snake
seasoned its muttering with a subtler truth.
Give up the tranquil gape of mouth and mind.
'Bite fervently and grow' is the apple's core.
And though with thorns, the hogweed's hug, the sweat
and groan of work, still grasp the heavy plough,
plant disappointment, harvest Paradise.

Angela Livingstone

And the man said, The woman whom thou gavest *to be* with me, she gave me of the tree, and I did eat.

Genesis 3: 12

Organic

Ah taste life here!
Grip on grapes.
Tell me about this red ...
     and bite.
Never walk past that green ...
     or neglect to lick.

Ish and *ishah*
– *ah* because she came out of him.
Ah ha the Hebrew
puns left
embedded.

Such excellent excesses:
     yellow banana,
     pomegranate pink
     fruit good to eat.
Ah – juice, just swallow it down.
Shshshshsh.

Big squishy.
Fig opening like thee.
Pear shaped body.
Thy peachiness.

Man and *woman*
– *wo*, because she came out of him?
O wow the English
turnaround right:
words untranslatable.

The garden indulges us.
Behold on wiggly branches
the most beautiful tree

has such wise fruit,
as irresistible as
breath.

Say 'ah'.
Oozy bite.
Eyes open.

'She gave me of the tree
and I did eat.'
Ssssssssssss in
rustling bushes.

Wo-ah!
To taste is to know
no.

Joan Norlev Taylor

And Cain talked with Abel his brother: and it came to pass, when they were in the field, that Cain rose up against Abel his brother, and slew him.
And the LORD said unto Cain, Where *is* Abel thy brother? And he said, I know not: *Am* I my brother's keeper?
And he said, What hast thou done? the voice of thy brother's blood crieth unto me from the ground.

Genesis 4: 8-10

Cain's Homecoming

The sun sets low beyond the western rim,
And, in the gloaming, footsore wanderers
Wonder where to wander now.
And he who walks among them walks alone
Ageless, worn down by waning wrath

'The fields lie fallow, and have done so since
 the day my brother breathed his last;
The flame of anger, unassuaged by grief or guilt
Burnt on for years
But now it's dull and ruddy,
Nothing but an ember
Of enmity long sated.

'And to you, my children
I can offer nothing;
The crops are burnt and gone –
Just another wasted gesture.
And would you kill the fatted calf for me,
My children's children's children,
When I darken your door in the shadow
Cast in the evening of the world?'

Keith Currie

And God looked upon the earth, and, behold, it was corrupt; for all flesh had corrupted his way upon the earth.

And God said unto Noah, The end of all flesh is come before me; for the earth is filled with violence through them; and, behold, I will destroy them with the earth.

Make thee an ark of gopher wood; rooms shalt thou make in the ark, and shalt pitch it within and without with pitch.

Genesis 6: 12-14

Ode to Free Schools
(after Frank O'Hara)

The education charity ARK, founded by a financier, is
spearheading the proposed academy in Wandsworth.

In the City

We shall have everything we want
multitudinous nannies in our nappy valley
and no more paying private school fees
for the symbol of our new Academy
will acknowledge vulgar materialism
and we will fill our insatiable privileged classrooms
with pupils from Honeywell Belleview High View
we like customers from homes with a view
who glide past closer catchments on lubricated
wheels of honey four by four
into our thirteen million pound ARK
our pupils milk lined satchels will inflate
with photographs of narcissists
and bankers and celebrities
like the neo tropic cormorant we dive
only for the shiniest fish
surfacing to flip and swallow head first
public cash raining down on us
like manna from heaven
for we are a free school and drawing breath
will take only a few
token two by two's into our ARK
for they are from the Winstanley Estate
on the wrong side of the Battersea tracks
it is the lay of the land

In the country

From the dizzy hilltop air
we shall see the free school renovation
rise near the churchyard elm
while from the sky a hook billed Gove
will circle and swoop to deliver the chosen few
out of the valley to bring them up unto
a good land a Stoke-by-Nay-land
where parents soak in granite baths
and intravenously graze on paupiettes of lemon soul
and from a council house imagination itself
will pedal a mountain bike boy
through the valley floor like an Olympian
flowing and covered with gold
but he will hesitate at the crossroads
see the golfer hole in one on the second course
the Constable country course
for he will know he will never hear
the music of their harps
or touch the four million pounds
reupholstered free school chair
he will ride back to his improving comprehensive
on tyre tread that does not roll on like a river
to stand with others on chipped classroom chairs
inserting fingers in holes of roofs
of never failing streams of rain water
and they will say in assembly
we have all things in common
we are of one heart and soul
take not our money let our people go

Mike Harwood

And the flood was forty days upon the earth; and the waters increased, and bare up the ark, and it was lift up above the earth.
And the waters prevailed, and were increased greatly upon the earth; and the ark went upon the face of the waters.

Genesis 7: 17-18

After the Flood

        And still the rain fell,
and it was hard to tell the day from night
since in the sky above was neither sun nor moon
and below were only black and rising waters
on which the little ark rocked back and forth,
God's toy on seas that now engulfed the earth.

His wine-stocks long-exhausted, Noah,
sober, quarrelled with his chiding wife,
the sons played up, and in the dismal dark
all cursed their confinement in the ark:
stink of animals was such to make them retch,
cries, hoots, bellows made perpetual din.
They couldn't open the one window wide
since so much driving rain came in.

Seasick, desperate, half-mad by now
they began to wish they had been drowned
along with all the rest of humankind,
cursed Noah as he sat there stony-faced
who was (he said) ordained by God to save them.
They knew not whether to believe him.

But then – a miracle – they found the rain had ceased
and the dove returned they'd days ago released,
bearing in its beak a branch of laurel,
so they knew the waters had at last abated.
As for the ark – that leaky overcrowded vessel,
so long buffeted about, found rest, and sat,
nudged against the sides of Ararat.

They lowered its door, and the inhabitants,
both animal and human, stumbled out
at first half-blinded by the sudden light
to meet a drowned and devastated world
that could as much have been another planet
than the plenteous earth they had once known.

They stood, bewildered and abashed. It was
only the rainbow in the sky – God's sign –
made them hope they could re-make it as their own.

Roger Caldwell

And Noah began *to be* an husbandman, and he planted a vineyard:
And he drank of the wine, and was drunken; and he was uncovered within his tent.
And Ham, the father of Canaan, saw the nakedness of his father, and told his two brethren without.
And Shem and Japheth took a garment, and laid *it* upon both their shoulders, and went backward, and covered the nakedness of their father; and their faces *were* backward, and they saw not their father's nakedness.

Genesis 9: 20-23

Noah, Naked and Pissed

Old people are my heroes
and I am right, and this is
why Yeats said old men should be mad
and Tennyson wrote 'Ulysses'
What virtue then in looking young
as is the media rule
when it's better to be foolish
and know that you're a fool?
Great age is not dignity –
that's for your middle age
neither is it dull wisdom
or lack of love or rage
when you know your onions
and you're sage

Noah, naked and pissed
post-ark, planted the vine
'not, surely, that same righteous man'
now in a flood of wine
But he still knew how to balance
the new world's rational fire
when the arrogance of youth
need douse its fierce desire
His sons who walked in backwards
with clothes to make him meeker
were more dumb and unnatural than
that ancient pisshead streaker
like Dionysus saving worlds
from being bleaker

Old folk defy the cliché
defy the ancient lie –
the fear that you project on them
that you will ossify
All the good old singers

they lose the flash of fashion
in voices now refined with age
and born of distillation
So, pissed or mad or setting out
to sea, for Happy Isle –
or jiving slowly in the sand
ignoring tides, meanwhile
they embrace what comes at last
with a strange smile

Not just Yeats and Tennyson
but Cadmus and Tiresias
going to the dance-athon
with Noah and with Ulysses
With Ulysses and Noah
and ourselves I can't ignore
capering, ludicrous ghosts we are
a final flap of dust to stir
this is what humans always were
and you could add your own, loud roar
to the venerable, vernal score
who cut a freak-out on the floor
who rave and fall upon the shore
who run or stagger to the door
to let strange angels in, and more
and make the young ashamed, I'm sure
that's what age is for

Adrian May

And it came to pass after these things, that God did tempt Abraham, and said unto him, Abraham: and he said, Behold, *here* I *am.*

And he said, Take now thy son, thine only *son* Isaac, whom thou lovest, and get thee into the land of Moriah; and offer him there for a burnt offering upon one of the mountains which I will tell thee of.

Genesis 22: 1-2

Sacrificing Children

After these things
this time, this stuff, this loss
and having no children –
in the offering of Isaac
the child is in us,
and those we never had
my love

The heart still keens
in the unborn world
for its increase
for the quickening of
its miracle

Suppress the honest
baby love talk
so we can walk in
the big world of
toddling adults
not making any
sacrifices

Testing and tempting
the endless deaths of
parents and children
within and without
and all are the testings
of ourselves

To grow and retreat
to embrace and renew
to remind us then
how to die and other
self-improvements

And my father is always
within me, like God
giving me life and death
Where else can he be?
Who else can I be?
The abandoned child
our only one whom
we lovest

And we cut the wood
and we take the journey
and we take the fire in our hand
and we take the knife
and we say Here I am
can I not be part of the divine
can I not be sacred
a sacrifice?

How else will we find blessing
more distant in our childless state
Outward jest, or good sense and yet like
solemn children?

But Isaac was the end of sacrifice
to say the sacred is all
about us and within us
How shall we remind ourselves
except in this death
life caught in
this thicket?

After these things
testing and tempting
lay not thine hand
upon the lad, the child
of your becoming
as each last offering
will be given
unbidden

Each made sacred as
childlessness is not then
an option, the sacred
will claim us, will make
us born

Into the wind
but not for the cruel end
or the cursed worst murder
or mere paradox
dead and alive
the King

But for the simple ritual
alive in all our
child's eyes
and in the impossible
loss and quickening
of love

Adrian May

Two nations *are* in thy womb, and two manner of people shall be separated from thy bowels; and *the one* people shall be stronger than *the other* people; and the elder shall serve the younger.

Genesis 25: 23

Rebekah

Already they were jostling within her –
one was a country of forest and moss,

bare feet pounding the earth.
Everything red-brown and sudden.

The other was open terrain, slippery
blue-grey. Water closing over,

no footprints left behind.
She composed her own map for each land.

Even the rain fell differently – it spattered
on trees or gashed against cliffs.

Through months she listened;
the two nations shared a language

yet the same word was a leaf
on one side, a pebble on the other.

She sensed a father-son and a mother-son.
How would she hold them together?

Could both be home or would one always
be in exile? She rested her palms

on their softness, their bones.
Twenty years of emptiness, and waiting –

all the love she'd stored would never
be enough to stave off a war.

Anne Ryland

And he commanded the steward of his house, saying, Fill the men's sacks *with* food, as much as they can carry, and put every man's money in his sack's mouth.

And put my cup, the silver cup, in the sack's mouth of the youngest, and his corn money. And he did according to the word that Joseph had spoken.

... And Joseph said unto them, What deed *is* this that ye have done? wot ye not that such a man as I can certainly divine?

Genesis 44: 1-2, 15

This is the Cup

'Such a man as I can certainly divine'
said Joseph, as uncertain as us
of his brothers
and divination was deemed an abomination

Testing, entrapping, tricky
like they'd been to him
hiding his cup in their bag

And the puritan, likewise, opens the Bible
at random to find an oracular verse
still as torn between belief and uncertainty

And I remember a friend consulting the *I Ching*
with a frivolous question, and he got an answer
that told him not to be so foolish

And another friend gave up fortune-telling
not for unbelief but for the loss to his spirit
in giving so much to those hesitant
believers who came to him

And sometimes when drunk
I can be serious enough
to read people with an unrestless power
blind to my own fate
like that time in Ireland

And there is an app for your phone
selecting a random Bible verse too
O the need for Something to talk to you

A seeking to test our sincerity
Can we ever be still and open enough
to divine the divine in us?

Timorous across the centuries
united in uncertainty
divided in our divination's
desire for the divine
dimidiated, diminished
we know we can only be real in
the fake and the faith of need

And the cup he drank from –
where in the water's reflection
or holding the air of the future
or reflecting the sun
or in the dropped stones' pattern
did he define the divine?

Is not this the cup of promise?
Is not this the container of uncertain hope
hidden in the sack of our burden of desire?
The grail, the vessel of grain, the vagina,
    nourishment, holding
the bitter suffering, unqualified thirsting
the elixir, the common cuppa, the lost quest
Is not this the cup of thyself the thief
being drawn thereby in mistrust of all
yet seeking foolish belief?

And you don't know if I got this last verse at random
attempting the serious moment
or smart-arse artist's careful con, faking much diviner
or if I, blind, picked it in the dark
groping for my future like all fools in pain –

'I hate vain thoughts …
I hope in thy word …
and let me not be ashamed of my hope'

Adrian May

And these *are they which* ye shall have in abomination among the fowls; they shall not be eaten, they *are* an abomination: the eagle, and the ossifrage, and the ospray.

Leviticus 11: 13

Sovereignty

some of them are as like the dietement of the Spirit of God,
as an Egg is to an Oyster – James VI, 'Basilikon Doron'

Her cry opens the first poem
in the first poetry anthology,
punning on fair for royal love
in the Chinese Book of Songs –
but on bed in common French,
for her page in my RSPB book.

Her Latin name's wrong myth;
late into English, then in error –
if she's taken by Shakespeare
on her 'sovereignty of nature',
King James' Authorised Version
loses her purity in translation.

Called fish eagle and sea hawk,
she is neither hawk nor eagle,
a genus unto herself as a law
whose spirit defeats all letters.
We guard her castle in this air,
its proper address also secret.

Ian Duhig

And when ye reap the harvest of your land, thou shalt not make clean riddance of the corners of thy field when thou reapest, neither shalt thou gather any gleaning of thy harvest: thou shalt leave them unto the poor, and to the stranger: I *am* the LORD your God.

Leviticus 23: 22

Corners

I can't decide whether Coleridge,
who loved to look at gates
in the corners of fields,
would have rejoiced at Leviticus 23
where *the Lord spake unto Moses*
saying *thou shalt not wholly reap*
the corners of thy field:
thou shalt leave them for the poor,
and for the stranger
or been slightly anxious
such a policy
might obscure his view.

David Charleston

At her feet he bowed, he fell, he lay down: at her feet he bowed, he fell: where he bowed, there he fell down dead.

Judges 5: 27

Jael

They came away from our mountain wars
slow with the effort of losing a country.
Foreign men, armour-hulked. Trudging, blood
on their pelts. Outsiders, and that blood
of a different making.

Animals. Kneeling to drink, dog-lipped.
Only one cupped his hands and stood. Proud
as the axis lords of Philistine. A leader,
used to strength. Though horses, men and everything
broken in the war's clumsy rout.
Half-dead with knock and shield-butt.

Foreign as locusts. Still, I called him
Majesty. Sheltered him, burned my lamps
after dark, the shouts of troops
far as Jerusalem,
while the clouds skittled rain
over the scree of Ephraim.

He slept here on my bed. I think he dreamed
of his country. Temples carved
with Baals, green-tongued. His god the demon
of noontide and scorching summers.

After, when Israel had won
its valleys and the high passes
for the goats, the orators made words of me.
They praised the power in my forehead
and my workers' hands, although
it wasn't hard to do. The tent-peg sharp,
new pine, tanned with sap.
The tenting mallet solid yew.

The foreigner sunk in his sleep,
mosquitoes settling like knives
on his lips and where lank hair
thinned at the temples' cradle-bone.
To pick the stake and judge the blow—

No work, that. A single breath.
Lighter shift than pressing wine,
or camping on the desert plain.
The men gone, and the tents to pitch.

No work. I daydream of a king's skull.
My strength, his strength, his death.
And my hands itch.

Tobias Hill

And Delilah said unto Samson, Hitherto thou hast mocked me, and told me lies: tell me wherewith thou mightest be bound. And he said unto her, If thou weavest the seven locks of my head with the web.

And she fastened *it* with the pin, and said unto him, The Philistines *be* upon thee, Samson. And he awaked out of his sleep, and went away with the pin of the beam, and with the web.

Judges 16: 13-14

eBible

Samsong read testaments electronic,
in general format, zipped Bible archives:
original, Wycliffe hotmail old, Tyndale hotmail new,
unified, medium, plain standard, bold.
Scrolling down he saw the time to die
prophesied at *the end dot com*,
alongside spam flashing vouchers for fat
tier double world wide web hamburgers,
and butler service at hotel Shangri-La.
Tempted by eBible bargains on sixty nine disks,
with XML scripture encoding facilities
and free electronic edge swords of the Lord,
Samsong's cursor hovered on 'add to my basket',
a speaking Bible at *lowcostshopper dot uk*.
But it came to pass, when the woman he loved, Dellia,
pressed him daily, that for her birthday she would
prefer a book, the King James Version Bible book.
For everything there is a reason; at six ninety nine
Samsong gave Dellia a KJV paperback,
appointed and authorised to be printed in China,
with space to write, presented by and date,
with room to turn and smell the freshness of the page,
with time to feel the rhythms pounding in the hand,
to hear the poetry of the enduring image,
to hold the KJV, echoing a drama for our age.

Mike Harwood

And she came to Jerusalem with a very great train, with camels that bare spices, and very much gold, and precious stones: and when she was come to Solomon, she communed with him of all that was in her heart.

1 Kings 10: 2

Sheba's Journey

I tried to conjure words to link
the Sheep Pool, goats' feet,
hairy legs, mica floor,
tried to re-assemble that iconic meeting,
Solomon and Sheba

and they were here, at the edge
of my eye the whole time I sat
unpicking that sonnet sequence,
studying the artefacts,
tracking Sheba's stories back

and what tracks she's left!
In Poynter's gallery painting, he's free
to bare her breasts
as long as there are pearls
to hang between.

Sheba as circus Queen, 1914,
all 'extravagance and splendor';
white thighs exposed behind
a golden drape, flanked
by peacocks in full flounce.

Lollobrigida herself,
in 'Solomon and Sheba';
twenty four versions of Dior
transparency, veiling something
low-rent and Neapolitan.

And on my wall, an Ethiopian in white
holds a palanquin above the pair;
locked into each other's dark gaze,
they clasp hands, their robes
royal reds and purples, trimmed with gold.

Pam Job

And they spake unto him, saying, If thou wilt be a servant unto this people this day, and wilt serve them, and answer them, and speak good words to them, then they will be thy servants for ever.

1 Kings 12: 7

Kings

Rehoboam shuts his ears to the masses
boiling around his pearly palace,
the talk of sanctions on the World Service,
at the UN the threat of frozen assets.

Our golden leader has learned from Solomon's
abasements – his whores, abominations
and follies – damns all his sons and grandsons
to chastise us not with whips, with scorpions.

Antony Dunn

Then Job answered and said,
I know *it is* so of a truth: but how should man be just with God?
If he will contend with him, he cannot answer him one of a thousand.

Job 9: 1-2

In the Land of Uz

The earth is shaken out of its place
and the pillars thereof tremble.

The sky shrouds tides and throws them up
as veils across the face of the thunder.

Hast thou entered into the springs of the sea
and caused the overflow of the waters

and the land to rise up as its dolphin self
and career on its back with the salt in its skin?

Yes, the doors of the sea are flung wide open
and the proud waves break over the world.

He maketh the sea to boil like a pot,
a foaming white tsunami, *a pot of ointment,*

to spread thick and black on landfall; a purging
of oceans vomited as flotsam strewn on land.

The bottles of heaven are emptied into water spouts
sucking in ships to sail on the ocean floor.

A cyclist pedals away down an empty road
while the sludge surges faster at his back.

They came upon me as a wide breaking in of waters,
in their devastation they rolled themselves upon me.

My harp is tuned to mourning, now the land is liquid
and the waves wear garlands of fire.

Pam Job

He maketh my feet like hinds' *feet,* and setteth me upon
my high places.

Psalm 18: 33

The voice of the Lord shaketh the wilderness; the Lord
shaketh the wilderness of Kadesh.
The voice of the Lord maketh the hinds to calve, and
discovereth the forests: and in his temple doth every
one speak of *his* glory.

Psalm 29: 8-9

Hinds' Feet

Like hinds' feet, narrow and cleft,
with ankles coiled and sprung
for the dancing, for bounding

over rocks and through trees,
for running up slopes and pivoting
on the summit: not like my feet at all

heavy-shod, thick and splayed
for the trudge along pavements,
the plod over tarmac, the march

upstairs and down. My old feet
broad-set to keep me rooted to the ground
aren't used to teetering,

the tiptoe stance of deer, the high
heeled strut, the ballet pirouette,
the toe-hold climb, the long jump.

I'm not good with heights, they make my palms
prickle and weaken my knees;
I need something to cling to. Yet love

has lifted me out of my sad
stiff self and for reasons best known
has set me here in the uplands,

in a wild and far-flung place
full of cloud and heather –
no shelter from changing weather.

Now lightfoot I wander
and lift my head to the wind
to listen for its direction.

The voice of the LORD shaketh the wilderness...
The voice of the LORD maketh the hinds to calve,
and discovereth the forests.

The trail I leave is slender, open
and curved like petals, female
as the horns of the moon.

Hilary Llewellyn-Williams

The LORD *is* my shepherd; I shall not want.
He maketh me to lie down in green pastures: he leadeth
me beside the still waters.

Psalm 23: 1

At the Baptism

The priest speaks of how in the West
we've lost all sense of symbols
while happy himself to mangle
the language of the 23rd Psalm
with *The LORD is my shepherd;*
There is nothing I shall want.

How as a child, in stultifying choir and Sunday school,
I had been happy to *lie down in green pastures,*
to be led *beside the still waters*
and yes, though I had never walked
through the valley of the shadow of death,
I feared *no evil.*

David Charleston

He restoreth my soul: he leadeth me in the paths of righteousness for his name's sake.

Yea, though I walk through the valley of the shadow of death, I will fear no evil: for thou *art* with me; thy rod and thy staff they comfort me.

Psalm 23: 3-4

Jacket

Finally, I see the colour consultant,
she tells me about the spectrum, decides
on midnight blue. The stars come out

during the day on this jacket. Her friends,
in jeans or worn corduroy, are lower down
the spectrum in pale blues or browns, yet

they are gentle as they strap between my legs,
pull tight across my chest. I fold my arms
to keep the lines clean. Once, at art college,

I saw a man wriggle clear of his; it was buckled
incorrectly. Mine is comfy, except when I think
wrong thoughts; then the stars ignite and fizz,

needle my blood. I'm told my imagination
leads me into temptation. I'm to relax.
A man takes me to dinner, spoons the soup,

smiles and wipes my chin. I ask if the jacket
matches my eyes. He asks if I'd like a shave.
He is in love, so are the rest. Even the consultant

glimpses something special in me, she gazes
through the glass, invites her corduroyed friends,
their eyes, their ears follow my every movement.

I grunt through my psalms, the valley of the shadow
of death. My palms start to itch. Yea, I shall think only
good thoughts, good thoughts, good thoughts …

Katrina Naomi

I will praise thee with my whole heart: before the gods will I sing praise unto thee.

Psalm 138: 1

The Resurrection of Gilbert Kaplan

I shall soar upwards to the light which no eye has penetrated! Rise again, yes, rise again: Mahler

As those closing bars gave way to a reverberating
silence, something long frozen within you thawed
like the ice floes of an Alpine river in spring sunlight.

You sensed that nothing would ever be the same
again after hearing that choir's voices soar as if to
assault the heavens and those last trumpets call from afar.

In everyone's life, perhaps, there are moments which
hold within themselves the promise of renewal but we
lack the courage to follow them wherever they might lead.

Moments like certain angles of light on a hill lochan
at evening when the sun gives up the ghost behind
stoned hills and sheep bleat to the rhythm of waves

slowly advancing and retreating, advancing and
retreating on bouldered shores; a moored lobster
boat rising and falling, rising and falling . . .

the stilled air weighted with salt and peat smoke evoking
memories one can't quite hold on to like the dark
water of a rushing burn which leaves faint traces

of itself on our chilled fingers. You, Gilbert , travelled
the earth in pursuit of one who *surrendered* himself
 to the music which was *dictated* to him like a man

who follows the urgent promptings of love and fate.
Your fixed your eyes on the motions of maestros;
you immersed yourself in that miraculous score

like a deep sea diver exploring the beds of oceans.
You became the symphony you dreamed of conducting
until, one day, your dream was fulfilled and music

flowed from your guided fingertips, your slim baton
conjouring decipherable patterns through air.
The symphony must be a world , said Mahler

and you recreated this glorious world with your own
rhythmic hands, carving unimaginable sounds
like a sculptor who frees the form within the stone.

Like you, we unknowingly long for something other:
for some rebirth of what we once possessed, our
voices, at last, answering that persistent echo within.

James Knox Whittet

Note:
The life of the Wall Street financier, Gilbert Kaplan, was
transformed by hearing Mahler's *Resurrection Symphony*.
Despite his limited musical knowledge, he eventually
achieved his dream by conducting and recording this
symphony which became the biggest selling Mahler
recording of all time.

And I gave my heart to seek and search out by wisdom concerning all *things* that are done under heaven: this sore travail hath God given to the sons of man to be exercised therewith.

Ecclesiastes 1: 13

In Memory of R. S. Thomas

I see you with your sparse locks of
greying hair lifted by sea winds as you
stand gazing skywards, your eyes following
the guided flight paths of sea birds.

Your past, a litany of place names:
Anglesey, Eglwys – fach, Manafon,
Aberdaron around which the haunting
images fold like burning birch leaves.

You knelt at the altars of stubborn,
stone churches on that borderland of doubt
and belief, your ears attuned to those moorland
silences in which that bewildering God resides.

Sometimes the plain words of your prayers
would ignite and an arrow of sunlight would
pierce the stained glass and painted figures
would move as if in an eternal dance

like the atoms in physicists' strange tables
in which solidity exists only in our minds.
Your footsteps echo no longer down those still
lanes of Lynn, scented with the dessicated coconut

of gorse and misted with the vapours of
cattle's breath rising from behind high hedges.
In remote cottages, the old would spin yarns of
loneliness in the slow treadmills of dreams.

Do you continue with your fierce questioning
now you've merged with your loved Welsh loam?
Or are your powdered ears tuned only to the sea's
slow intakes of breath on nights pillared with frost

when willow wands of smelted moonlight cradle
Ynys Enlli which lies just out of reach, as
always, across the Sound where the ghosts of dead
saints step through green seas of lush grass?

Your ashes lie just outwith the church you
could never wholly enter as you explored that
adult geometry of the mind where acute angles
dissected angles like your wife's intricate veins.

God's rebellious angel, you placed words like
stepping stones to bridge the gaps between
islands of meaning which float in vast oceans
over which a watered rainbow sometimes arcs.

James Knox Whittet

As the apple tree among the trees of the wood, so *is* my beloved among the sons. I sat down under his shadow with great delight, and his fruit *was* sweet to my taste.
He brought me to the banqueting house, and his banner over me *was* love.
Stay me with flagons, comfort me with apples: for I *am* sick of love.

Song of Solomon 2: 3-5

Comfort Me with Apples

Beware their shiny cheeks;
the curl of peel spelling out her name.

Beware their bite;
the taste of flesh, the sweetness of her breath.

Build me towers of every kind of apple,
lock the harvest away.

Beware the sun,
for I can only countenance night.

Bid me drink from rotten fruits
whose juice has turned to spirit –

only then shall you comfort me with apples,
for I am sick of love.

Katrina Naomi

Who hath believed our report? and to whom is the arm of the LORD revealed?

For he shall grow up before him as a tender plant, and as a root out of a dry ground: he hath no form nor comeliness; and when we shall see him, *there is* no beauty that we should desire him.

He is despised and rejected of men; a man of sorrows, and acquainted with grief.

Isaiah 53: 1-3a

The Secret Starer

Observe still life intently for long periods of time
without fearing ridicule, embarrassment, intimidation,
hostility.

Steady scrutiniser, private
ogler, look-kissed and caressed,

getting to know, hold,
fondle, thus acquainted

with grief, with joy,
warmth, the abundant arcs,

curves of the human shape
in its changing, seen in what

we make and shape: *stay me*
with flagons, arabesques of arms,

luscious handle undulation,
pout of jug-spout.

Robert Vas Dias

The harvest is past, the summer is ended, and we are not saved.

Jeremiah 8: 20

The light of the body is the eye: if therefore thine eye be single, thy whole body shall be full of light.

Gospel of Matthew 6: 22

Mountain Bikers

How long will it go on –
the lurch of the ski-lift
though mist,
the two of us and a child
suspended under power-lines?

Our bodies lightsome
in this kingdom
of the negligible,
only cow-bells sounding
the invisible beasts.

Then we glimpse them –
eerie bikers, also going up
without horizons,
their machines
slung from the gondola

an oddly muted
travelling circus,
their aero-dynamic helmets
heraldic, under the unseen
stations of the sun

stranger than Odin's ravens
flying between past
and future
above the calamitous ground
where we are not saved.

Pauline Stainer

The hand of the LORD was upon me, and carried me out in the spirit of the LORD, and set me down in the midst of the valley which *was* full of bones.

Ezekiel 37: 1

Life of Bones

It is a hard life,
with bones under you.
— Diane Wakoski, 'The Helms Bakery Man'

It is a forgiving life with bones under you
        you're not conscious of,

backbone unstooped, legs swinging
        on the walk without pain.

Bones feel hard but aren't, they're tender,
        bruise, throb, need cushioning

by disc, meniscus, cartilage
        to stop them from wearing

us down. It's the pain wears us away
        when the knee won't flex in the dance.

A life with bones
        is deceptively hard, but not

as hard as dry bones unclothed
        when flesh is not upon them

and the marrow in its narrow
        channels leaches out,

makes not blood nor poetry
        but leaves the hollows for others

to breathe their songs into,
        dry bones to bang the drum.

Robert Vas Dias

So they took up Jonah, and cast him forth into the sea: and the sea ceased from her raging.

Now the LORD had prepared a great fish to swallow up Jonah. And Jonah was in the belly of the fish three days and three nights.

Jonah 1: 15, 17

Jonah in the Whale

On the first day
Jonah sat in the
Darkness, thinking
Here I am safe
From the Lord,
And I have
Plenty to eat,
Even if I am not
Fond of krill.

*

On the first night,
Though it was
Indistinguishable
From the day,
Jonah ate three
Raw herrings,
Cutting his mouth
On the sharp bones.
He began to
Wonder how he
Might escape.

*

On the second day,
Though it was
Indistinguishable
From the night,
Jonah grew thirsty
And drank the soup
In the whale's belly.
Sooner or later, he
Thought, the whale

Will vomit me out,
For I am an old
And indigestible man.

*

On the second night,
Though it was
Indistinguishable
From the day,
Jonah was sorely sick,
And for the first
Time began to
See the folly of fleeing
The presence of the Lord.
There was a loud bump
As the whale rested
On the ocean floor.

*

On the third day,
Though it was
Indistinguishable
From the night,
Jonah fed on the
Krill which now
Surrounded him
Up to the chest.
He felt faint and wished
In himself to die.
This was much worse
Than a day passed
Preaching doom to the
People of Nineveh,
He thought.

*

On the third night,
Though it was
Indistinguishable
From the day,
Jonah prayed to
The Lord, surrounded
By krill which now
Rose all the way
To his neck.
'I will pay that
I have vowed,'
He gurgled.

*

On the fourth day,
Which was a day
Of warm sunshine,
The Lord spake unto
The whale and it
Vomited Jonah out
On dry land.
Jonah sat in the sun
To dry out, watching
The women of Nineveh
Lying on the beach.
The children pointed
At him and laughed,
Wondering if he was
A man or a fish.

Philip Terry

Out of him came forth the corner, out of him the nail, out of him the battle bow, out of him every oppressor together.

And he shall pass through the sea with affliction, and shall smite the waves in the sea, and all the deeps of the river shall dry up: and the pride of Assyria shall be brought down, and the sceptre of Egypt shall depart away.

Zechariah 10: 4, 11

Mighty Men

Archers with bows tensed, hovering hawks,
caparisoned horses, tassels flying;
leaders with spears poised for skewering,
short swords unsheathed.

Steeds in pursuit, mouths spittling on bits,
manes plaited; riders with braided hair,
with soft-laced boots, pound their horses flanks
spurring them on.

They have captured Ummanaldash!
The King of Elam is taken!
He is in the war chariot among the flowers and flocks
and the hawks are diving down.

A soldier grasps his hand in the tight clasp
of the conqueror, another pulls his beard.
They are opening his mouth, showing his teeth
and his army cover their heads in shame.

Pam Job

And there were in the same country shepherds abiding in the field, keeping watch over their flock by night.

And, lo, the angel of the Lord came upon them, and the glory of the Lord shone round about them: and they were sore afraid.

And the angel said unto them, Fear not: for, behold, I bring you good tidings of great joy, which shall be to all people.

Gospel of Luke 2: 8-10

Christmas Letter

We flock to buy cards.
A Christmas letter is begun.
As with choirs of angels, we send good
tidings of great joys,
tidying into brighter parcels
our straying, night-watched lives.
We come to the yearly fold,
beholding on this day our highest
moments – because the spirit of Christmas is glad,
and tinsel-sparkling.

And so we sing
of heavenly holidays, white weddings,
friends and children, a baby's birth,
as lights shining in the darkness.
And thus we sound our celebration
of salvation, voicing praises of perfect
events, asking for a new song
of hallelujahs to our success
and all things good,
with nothing wrong.

Let that be understood; this is a mustered song.
No one walks these muddy hills in cotton wool,
braying for sheepish congratulations.
See how we shove the deepest shadows
into corners of untold stories,
to turn away to stars and trumpet
glory: the brighter sides,
to share with those we love, hoping
they will echo and sing out new refrains,
as a gleaming chain.

See us place our silver linings,
as if we know no hell,
as if the grazed life
we have is always play.
Unto us was born this day
a simple tune of love we sometimes hear.
And so, in chorus
with those field-framed angels,
we sound our little earthly bells
and wish each other well.

Joan Norlev Taylor

In the beginning was the Word, and the Word was with God, and the Word was God.

Gospel of John 1: 1

For where two or three are gathered together in my name, there am I in the midst of them.

Gospel of Matthew 18: 20

In Latter Days

After two or three
had gathered in His name,

the purring began.
Showers of bright semi-quavers
and the mountains skipped,
floods clapped their hands.

In the great emptiness,
on your knee-bones,
you dreamed about decay
and holy mildew
all over chiming England.

Again we sang;
then an officer trundled up
to the savage lectern
with his babyfood bible.

O ye gods…

Divine authority,
our fathers' cadences,
and their fathers' fathers,
shuffled off.

Committee-speak!
The work of the worthy
with flat feet,
fearful of fire and unknowing.

In the terrible gloom
you lowered your head,
accomplice
while the Word
was betrayed by the word.

Kevin Crossley-Holland

And why take ye thought for raiment? Consider the lilies of the field, how they grow; they toil not, neither do they spin.

Gospel of Matthew 6: 28

After Long Fallow

It's an orthodox insight –
every seventh year
the land must lie fallow,
even the river
go underground.

Beyond the lilies of the field,
little animals
lean into the wind
as if listening
to its subsong

while we wait
for that rekindling
which conjures
a blue abstract
out of the flaxfield.

Pauline Stainer

For Herod himself had sent forth and laid hold upon John, and bound him in prison for Herodias' sake, his brother Philip's wife: for he had married her.

Gospel of Mark 6: 17

Consequences – A partly-found poem

The prisoner, *a just man and an holy*,
was brought before the king. The king *observed him*
with some trepidation;
the fellow had already said too much
yet when he talked the king still *heard him gladly*.

This prisoner whose words *did many things* –
including taking royalty to task –
had caused grave consternation
when he'd told the king '*It is not lawful*
to have thy brother's wife.' The queen was cross.

The king was scared of her and changed the subject.
Thinking *a convenient day was come*
to have a celebration
he *made a supper to his lords, high captains*
(and assorted others) *on his birthday*.

The daughter of the queen *came in and danced*
which pleased the king *and them that sat with him*.
For this titillation
he swore 'I'll give thee *whatsoever thou*
shalt ask of me ... unto half my kingdom.'

The queen did not forget she *had a quarrel*
with the prisoner. She *would have killed him*
but, to her frustration,
could not find a way to move *against him*
till her daughter asked '*What shall I ask?*'

She told her, 'Go *straightway with haste,* insisting
that your heart desires the prisoner's head.
Demand decapitation;
give me by and by the evidence;
and when you bring it, bring it *in a charger.*'

The king *would not reject her, for his oath's sake*
and for those *which sat with him.* His head,
protecting reputation,
sent an executioner (although
his heart already was *exceeding sorry*).

Thereafter any rabbi stirring rumours –
mighty works shew forth themselves in him –
increased his agitation:
'Could this him be him *whom I beheaded*
come to haunt me, *risen from the dead*?'

Michael Bartholomew-Biggs

And there shall be signs in the sun, and in the moon, and in the stars; and upon the earth distress of nations, with perplexity; the sea and the waves roaring.

Gospel of Luke 21: 25

Waves

Still dream of body-
        surfing crests of waves
ecstasy of hoist and thrust
        in foam-rush pummel
to the skin-scraping shore
        when my mouth issued sea
ears roaring with it
        spray spumed breath.

                Numberless
summer afternoons we boys met
        out where they began to break,
ducked under the not-quite-big-enough
        to lure the nearly perfect
seventh to furl us in
        its breaking coil, tumble us
into its foaming race.

                Now age
cautions, body's
        inflexibility prevents desire
to bend before that capricious
        power, I imagine
broken bones, or worse.

                The sea's surge
has shifted sandbanks, flung flotsam
        up the beach, re-jigged the coastline,
breached defences
        the dream become Sendai,
Aceh tsunami nightmare,
        lofting houses off foundations,

cars, boats, bodies tossed
in black waters, reduced
to debris, *upon the earth
distress of nations, with perplexity;
the sea and the waves roaring.*

Robert Vas Dias

Now in the morning as he returned into the city, he hungered.
And when he saw a fig tree in the way, he came to it, and found nothing thereon, but leaves only, and said unto it, Let no fruit grow on thee henceforward for ever. And presently the fig tree withered away.

Gospel of Matthew 21: 18-19.

Let no fruit grow on thee...

& when he came to it

it was in spate – as though
a river green with
swelling had

halted & stood
up in itself or some
white sea had swung there

a green hull creaking
with its swell of
fruit & he

stood in that
wide shade hungered
seeing side by side two

purpled fruit blushed &
strained with summer
he took them

split them
drank that sweetness
of a tree so long expectant

as one gold drop slunk
from his lip it came
upon him so

deep he moved
away from them &
leaning forward rested

one smooth palm on that
smooth grey trunk
& swallowing

his half
-seeded curse for two
moments & with all before him

forgot himself

Mario Petrucci

And when the hour was come, he sat down, and the twelve apostles with him.

And he said unto them, With desire I have desired to eat this passover with you before I suffer:

For I say unto you, I will not any more eat thereof, until it be fulfilled in the kingdom of God.

Gospel of Luke 22: 14-16

Last Supper

In a room running on empty
you're painting your last Last Supper,
sailing wildscape waves of office hours,

sketching out five or six Januaries
before attempting February,

gambling on the colour blue,
the entire devilry of green.

How you loved the houses of one street,
all that's left of your applewood days.

Is it still light outside?
Shall we walk to the river?
Good enough medicine for anyone, you once said,
the miracle of watching simple water.

Penelope Shuttle

And they crucified him, and parted his garments, casting lots.

And sitting down they watched him there;

And set up over his head his accusation written, THIS IS JESUS THE KING OF THE JEWS.

Now from the sixth hour there was darkness over all the land unto the ninth hour.

And about the ninth hour Jesus cried with a loud voice, saying, Eli, Eli, lama sabachthani? that is to say, My God, my God, why hast thou forsaken me?

Jesus, when he had cried again with a loud voice, yielded up the ghost.

Now when the centurion, and they that were with him, watching Jesus, saw the earthquake, and those things that were done, they feared greatly, saying, Truly this was the Son of God.

Gospel of Matthew 27: 35a, 36-37, 45-46, 50, 54

The Centurion

He, centurion from Rome whose task it was
to supervise the grisly scene
at the place they called Golgotha,
was curious from the first about this man
chosen to be crucified between two thieves
in the place of murderous Barabbas.

This 'King of the Jews' was an enigma,
and the words he uttered in his agony –
'Father, forgive them for they know not
what they do' much troubled him.

What manner of man is this, he thought,
to merit such vituperation?
Why this crown of thorns?
It was in great wonderment he stayed and watched.

Skies darkened from the sixth hour onwards,
and it was only when the ninth hour came
did this man cry out that 'It is finished' –
his head dropped, he gave up the ghost,
now a mere wrecked body on a wooden cross.

But then he, the Roman, listened out and felt
a trembling in the earth, and in the skies above
a sigh went up, as if of something gone
that never would return again
as it had been before.

        And went his way,
slow-footed, back towards Jerusalem,
uttering underneath his breath

words so odd, so strange to him
who had no faith – as if his world had changed
by all that he had heard and seen – 'In truth
this man could only be the son of God.'

Roger Caldwell
Good Friday, 2011

Now when the centurion saw what was done, he glorified God, saying, Certainly this was a righteous man.

Gospel of Luke 23: 47

Long Friday

1

Small sun through mist,
five turbines in silverpoint
blades turning, turning,
a swish as of walking
through long grass.

then the eerie shift
of something unfinished,
flicker-shadow,
the unco-ordinated wounds
of Christ.

2

Crucifixion,
a centurion
gazing up at the body
with its crown
of razor-wire

transfixed by
that shimmer
in zero-sunlight –
incarnation,
the dove

in the double helix.

Pauline Stainer

And when the Sabbath was past, Mary Magdalene, and Mary the *mother* of James, and Salome, had brought sweet spices, that they might come and anoint him.
And very early in the morning the first *day* of the week, they came unto the sepulchre at the rising of the sun.

Gospel of Mark 16: 1-2

There were giants in the earth in those days.

Genesis 6: 4

Gospel Truths I: Giants in Those Days

They shadowed every day, their stories closer,
realer than the news. Holy sandals scuffed
pavements, crunched the cindertrack to Golgotha.
The seaside's flatness was a Galilee ready
to erupt in storm, transfiguring the Lincolnshire
afternoon, their footprints inch by inch
disappearing in the slick anonymous sand.

I could reach out to touch them all – Peter
with his hot eyes and promises, John
leaning on God's shoulder, Mark running
through the olive-scented night in panic,
leaving his garment behind. In the dark a star
hung blinking over our shed, or a cock crew
from a neighbour's henhouse down the street.

It was not for a long time that I felt the absence
of women. There were some in the margins –
     anonymous,
asking for crumbs, bleeding, breaking their phial
of ointment, lying sick, raised from the dead
or waiting, dumbly, for stoning. A few had a name
but several Marys, it seemed, had been confused.
I was told this did not matter. They had their part.

Over the years the heroic footprints filled
with sea, lost their shape, faded at last
washed out by newer tides. The shining fish
slipped through the miracle net or, heaped
on the shore, grew dull, stank. Only the women's
voices rose now and then from the page
asking what it had all been for.

Christine Webb

And Jesus answered and said unto her, Martha, Martha, thou art careful and troubled about many things:
But one thing is needful: and Mary hath chosen that good part, which shall not be taken away from her.

Gospel of Luke 10: 41-42

Gospel Truths III: Martha

I was elbow-deep in grease. That lamb
(in a herb crust) doesn't exactly cook
itself. And there's a pan to scour after.
Then the home-made bread, bitterleaf salad
(lightly dressed with oil) not to mention
figs, plums, apricots, almonds and a couple
of bottles of wine. I didn't notice him
(or anyone) refusing second helpings
nor minding me dodging about with dishes,
spooning gravy, cutting extra bread.
After dinner, there's our Mary sitting
literally at his feet – he has the one
comfortable chair, she's hunched on a cushion
drinking it all in. I'm doing a quick sweep
round the kitchen, hoping to get back to the chat
half listening to them while I go on stacking
pots. Then here he is in the doorway:
'Mary's made the best choice,' he says.
I stare. Is this a joke? My good lamb
hardly out of his mouth, beard stained with gravy:
'You should prioritise more. Don't spend so long
in the kitchen.' And he's on his way,
picking a thread of meat from his teeth. God.

Christine Webb

Then took they the body of Jesus, and wound it in linen clothes with the spices, as the manner of the Jews is to bury.

Now in the place where he was crucified there was a garden; and in the garden a new sepulchre, wherein was never man yet laid.

There laid they Jesus therefore because of the Jews' preparation *day*; for the sepulchre was nigh at hand.

Gospel of John 19: 40-42

Gospel Truths V: Seeing Things

All the water in my body had run out
by the time he died. At first
I couldn't look at all, just kept my eyes
fixed on the little ridges my feet
had scuffed in the stained dust. But the shadow
fell on my bent neck like the sun, so
hot I had to look up. Then I was consumed
in looking: the muscles at full stretch, bones
edged as if they'd score the skin, the face
unrecognisable, eyes and mouth holes punched
into emptiness. And the hands (my hands
remembered their touch) splintered, pulped.
Couldn't look again. Had to. It got dark
but still hot. Dry thunder. The earth shook.
The end was a long time coming.

Interlude of good smells. Cave-smell, earthy
and cold. Winding the steeped bandages, sharp,
resinous. Walking away, the grass aromatic
with sap and dew. No tears: the stone
– its smell heavy, dense, neutral – had sealed
me up too.

Now the city is full of rumours, visions
multiplying like an infection. The men
are feverish, gathering, shouting in hoarse
excitement. I keep away. I too

had my moment of ecstasy, meeting
a dream in the long grass at dawn –
that tricky light when trees look like men
walking. He came towards me from the edge
of the sunrise.
       But it was only the gardener.

Christine Webb

But Jesus stooped down, and with *his* finger wrote on the ground, *as though he heard them not.*

Gospel of John 8: 6.

Love Letters in Dust

You wrote mysterious words on the shifting
dust of time whose meaning was lost
in rain and in the night winds of the desert.

You left no book to guide us, only a few
remembered words engraved on the hearts of
your listeners like the words cut by *a chisel*

*dipped in acid.** Those words, captured like
butterflies floating on scented, summer breezes
in the woven net of human language, are all

that remain, scrawled on rolls of papyrus, bleached
by sunlight and time, years after you had gone and
had returned from the nowhere and everywhere

from whence you came. Humans have lived and
suffered by the terrible power of this hearsay.
It's as if you did not wish your words to be

fixed forever in a book of your own writing where
each letter is nailed to the cross of a final meaning
but for the words to be deciphered through the currents

of the years, to be sculpted like olive wood so that they
take on the shape of the minds of those who have spoken
and loved them: the meaning is in the speaking and in

the loving. Believers have died with your recorded words
on their cracked and swollen lips. Monks have blinded
themselves in chilled, candle-lit scriptoriums where
   smoke

shadows scrawled altering apparitions across caved
walls, their ink seeping like shed blood into vellum.
Your spoken words have been illumined with silver and
   gold.

Those inspired scholars, chosen by King James,
wrote simple, earthbound words which soared into
flight like eagles across the poetry of starlit skies.

But perhaps it's not in the words in which your
deepest truths lie but in the silent spaces between:
if I listen closely, I can hear those whispers of eternity

like some gentle finger caressing love letters in dust.

James Knox Whittet

There is only a single reference to Jesus writing
throughout the whole of the Gospels and that is in St.
John: Chapter 8, Verse 6..
* Boris Pasternak.

And when he had thus spoken, he shewed them *his* hands and *his* feet.

And while they yet believed not for joy, and wondered, he said unto them, Have ye here any meat?

And they gave him a piece of a broiled fish, and of an honeycomb.

And he took *it*, and did eat before them.

Gospel of Luke 24: 40-43

Cleopas

I gave him broiled fish and a honeycomb
when he asked for meat.

    Oh, Lord! if he asked a fish, would I serve
    a *serpent*, for shame?

I first was hooked from my tears by the snap
of bread in his hands.

    My eyes were holden all the while the truth
    stared me in the face.

Antony Dunn

But Thomas, one of the twelve, called Didymus, was not with them when Jesus came.

The other disciples therefore said unto him, We have seen the Lord. But he said unto them, Except I shall see in his hand the print of the nails, and put my finger into the print of the nails, and thrust my hand into his side, I will not believe.

Gospel of John 20: 24-25

Knowledge

i. Eve

There was nothing to do but eat,
dress the bower with flowers,
touch flesh to the same flesh; vanilla skin.

Adam named things. It kept him amused.
Doltish beasts with flies in their lashes were 'cows'.
The 'goat' chewed and shat.

Water tinkled bland stones
and the sweet, looping song of birds wouldn't end.
Be fruitful, He said, *multiply and subdue*.

Eve spat pips one by one in the dust;
Adam's hand dandled her breast.
She did not know grief or sweat, but knew something.

ii. Abraham

I am simply following orders.
It is not for me to question.
These are my instructions.

I have surrendered to my fate.
He is all-knowing.
He says it must be done.

It is not for me to question.
I would be punished.
This is the Law.

.

I lift my eyes and see the place,
I lead the child
who carries wood,

who says: where *is* the lamb
for a burnt offering?
I talk of things provided,

there is a pyre. I push.
A knife lifts then shakes
aglitter; snot; that bleat;

but I am just the knife,
its faith in the hand,
and I must –

iii. Thomas

They shut the door.
Jesus breathed on them.
Jesus showed them his hand.
Thomas thrust fingers
in Jesus' side.
But blessed are those who have not seen,
and yet believe.
Blessed are those
who believe what they're told.

Clare Pollard

Simon Peter saith unto them, I go a fishing. They say unto him, We also go with thee. They went forth, and entered into a ship immediately; and that night they caught nothing.

Gospel of John 21: 3

Dawn Catch

We've got to get our heads round this. Would we
have stopped things going so far wrong
if we'd not run away? And can we
never put things right because we did?

Pete's the first one to admit he can't
be doing with it; flings himself
outside. We follow. Same old nets
and same old selves are waiting, know their job;
but now we're trawling for forgetfulness

it's no surprise we fetch up nothing.
Morning sun fills eyes with red
false copies of itself and hides a voice
that's pointing out the blinding obvious –
no fish – and saying try again.

Who does know-all think he is?
grunts Pete – but chucks the net out anyway.
At once the bulging thing's all fins and scales;
then someone says *It's him*. The next
we know we're waist-deep in the lake.

We strain ahead of dragging legs to reach him
then can't say a blessed word. We're out
of puff for one thing; and our mouths
are empty as our growling guts.
We fetch some of the catch for him to bake.

Does a breakfast on the beach with him
cross out the fact we let him down?
We don't dare ask – Pete least of all,
though he should be the first who gets to know.

Michael Bartholomew-Biggs

And there was a certain disciple at Damascus, named Ananias; and to him said the Lord in a vision, Ananias. And he said, Behold, I *am here*, Lord.

And the Lord *said* unto him, Arise, and go into the street which is called Straight, and inquire in the house of Judas for *one* called Saul, of Tarsus: for behold, he prayeth.

And hath seen in a vision a man named Ananias coming in, and putting *his* hand on him, that he might receive his sight.

Then Ananias answered, Lord, I have heard by many of this man, how much evil he hath done to thy saints in Jerusalem.

Acts of the Apostles 9: 10-13

Damascus Incident

No-one said I'd have to be a hero,
walk straight into trouble, run my head
into a noose.
        'What do you think you're playing,
        Lord?' I said (respectfully – assuming
        this was Him indeed and not some sudden
        unsuspected self-destructive quirk
        of mine). 'I venture in the lion's den
        (to coin a phrase) and, if not gobbled up
        at once, I heal the lion with bare hands?
        Then perhaps get eaten?'
                What a choice.
                Arrest or abject failure. Go to bed
                and sort it out tomorrow, Ananias.

Have you noticed He's persistent? Always
has an answer. And a good one too.
The one called Saul (it's Paul these days, I hear,
but he's the man) was waiting. So I scrambled
out my message in one breath.
        The lot:
        I called him brother; gave him my credentials;
        spelled out the situation; said I'd come
        to fix his eyesight ; promised him he'd see
        a whole new Spirit fill his life. (Don't ask
        me where I got that part.)
                God didn't dawdle
                either: when I touched him, problems fell
                away before my eyes –
                        and his as well of course.

Michael Bartholomew-Biggs

Nevertheless neither is the man without the woman, neither the woman without the man, in the Lord.
For as the woman *is* of the man, even so *is* the man also by the woman; but all things of God.

1 Corinthians 11: 11-12

for a newborn son

my hand cups

headbulb
shallowly planted
by blanket fine-haired

cheek versus palm its
tiny short-lived
shocks

of sap little
god in seven days
you have doubled folded

-mother intofather how
first crocus folds
spring from

flushwhite
fuse entering
winter reneging

soiled sleep taking
it new space
bubbled

white in
still dark you
float through un-

attached

Mario Petrucci

And I saw in the right hand of him that sat on the throne a book written within and on the backside, sealed with seven seals.

Revelation 5: 1

Revelator

The time has come and we are not prepared.
We are the dead-to-life that none can raise.
We are the beasts turned from the ark, unpaired.
We howl that this is not the end of days.

Antony Dunn

And I saw a new heaven and a new earth: for the first heaven and the first earth were passed away.

Revelation 21: 1

Liverpool Street Apocalypse

At Liverpool Street Station this afternoon I saw a forest:
a future and a past of wild woods sprawling, no sharp
brick noise, walls of traffic, and graffiti maze but
a stand of oak, the gentle sway of willows skirting streams,
sheltering green beneath the grey dabbing of rain.

On the Clacton train, going back to sleep, drooping, mute,
I saw concrete columns turn to trunks and boughs and all,
as I passed, change – become a past and the shape of things
to come. Our random fire of civilisation was just a simple
break in forest preceding and succeeding.

On railway sidings, cleared and gravelled, sentry weeds
already sprung, oblivious to our operations, careless of our
nomenclature, and trees grew like hands wiggling up from
beneath, confident in earth far deeper than our thin cover,
fingering wheels and tracks and signals.

Stratford steel cranes I saw turn to dust; Olympian designs
were rust below tendrils that even now invaded roofs, fences,
secretly taking over as our constructive eyes were turned.
Everywhere, they shot through cracks. Already the axe
is laid down at the foot of the trees.

Parks rimmed with asphalt roads became armies of bushes
wielding fruit and seeds. Tall stems pushed from ground
and unravelled into leaves and branches. Brick and iron, pvc
doors and windows – all obliterated under undergrowth,
crumbling into soil and worm earthworks.

We became the compost of the future.
At Liverpool Street Station one afternoon I saw a forest
as if the memory of the past lies imprinted on the present,
like a skeleton leaf on clay.

Joan Norlev Taylor

The Street of the Old Translators

The old crow clerics
Who haunt these narrow streets
In mildewed gowns

Would call this Sin,
What they are doing now,
Behind that window;

The room ill-lit, and low
And very old, tucked in
Beneath the eaves, crow-nest,

Sparrow-haunt; the street
Clattering below it;

Would name them – innocent
Of the world's commerce
And bustle – Sinners.

Those sour old priests would damn
Them to hell. And what for?

Because it will not translate.

Because these sentenced
Bodies articulate
Whatever is not body.

Out of the cloistered room
Into a limitless
Silence they trespass.

How terrible it is.

It can take years,
Forever, perhaps, to cross
Back to the street, its traffic.

Those poor clerics.
What did they know
Of the body's worship? –

Those porters, their business
To police the gates
And thresholds of heaven

From which no one has ever
Returned, or not quite?

Katrina Porteous

Battle of the Acronyms

I am KJB the King James Bible,
the world's greatest selling book.
I am JCB Joseph Cyril Bamford,
global producer of reversible plate
compactors and dumpsters, JCB.
I am KGM Kimberley Gold Mines.
I am KMG highest prices paid for silver, gold.
I am KPMG tax audit advice strategies
increasing profits in one hundred
and forty six countries, KPMG.
I am GMB employees need me, GMB.
I am BSkyB global news domination, BSkyB.
I am KGB Committee for State Security,
Komitet Gosudarstvennoy Bezopasnosti.
I am KGMB Keep Greater Milwaukee Beautiful.
We are the KGB King Ginsburg and Bartley,
playing fiddle tunes infiltrated by foreign agents
on Mole Records Seattle, band of three.
No, I am KGB exclusive daily deals
on fitness classes, massage, KGB.
I am JVC, unveiling the world's
first Consumer Camcorder with full HD;
capture that moment, life's no rehearsal.
I am AV the Authorized Version,
400 years of King James KJV,
quotable, distinctive, diverse, universal.

Mike Harwood

VOICES

Fleur Adcock was born in New Zealand but has lived in England since 1963. Her previous collections of poetry, now out of print, have been replaced by *Poems 1960-2000* (Bloodaxe, 2000), and a new collection, *Dragon Talk*, appeared in May 2010 (Bloodaxe). She has also published translations from Romanian and medieval Latin poetry, and edited several anthologies, including *The Faber Book of 20th Century Women's Poetry*. In 2006 she was awarded the Queen's Gold Medal for Poetry. In the course of researching her family history she discovered that she is descended from Dr Robert Tighe, one of the translators of the Bible and the subject of her poem in this anthology.

Michael Bartholomew-Biggs is a mathematician, now retired, who lives in Islington, where he is a co-organiser of the reading series Poetry in the Crypt. He has published several poetry collections of which the latest is *Tradesman's Exit* (Shoestring Press, 2009). For more information see www.poetrypf.co.uk.

Roger Caldwell was born in St Albans, and grew up in Hertfordshire. He worked for the British Council when the Iranian Revolution was brewing, and has also lived and taught in Canada and Germany. He has written on philosophy for journals such as *Philosophy Now*, on science and world politics for *Planet*, on music for *London Magazine* as well as contributing as a critic and reviewer of poetry to the *TLS, P.N. Review* and *Poetry Review*. His poetry has appeared in journals in the UK, USA, Canada, and New Zealand. His latest collection, *Waiting for World 93*, has recently appeared from Shoestring Press.

David Charleston has published two books of poems, *Nothing Better To Do* (Jardine Press, 1999) and *Small Parcel of Bones* (Happy Dragons' Press, 2008). A limited edition of nine poems entitled *Next-to-Nothing*, with photographs by Jessica Charleston, is being published by Shed Press Publications later in 2011. After teaching for a number of years, he is leaving to open a second-hand bookshop called The Open Road in September 2011 in Stoke-by-Nayland, Suffolk.

Enitharmon Press will publish **Kevin Crossley-Holland**'s *The Mountains of Norfolk: New and Selected Poems*, later this year. He is a translator from Anglo-Saxon, a broadcaster, and a well-known author for children. His most recent books are a memoir of childhood, *The Hidden Roads,* and the first of his Viking sagas, *Bracelet of Bones*, both published by Quercus. He is an Honorary Fellow of St. Edmund Hall, Oxford, and a Fellow of the Royal Society of Literature.

Keith Currie is currently studying for a PhD in literature at the University of Essex. He has been composing poetry in earnest since 2005, and has been actively performing his work as part of the university's Poetry Project since 2008. In September 2010 he performed several of his poems on the spoken word and comedy stage at the Liberty Festival in Trafalgar Square, an event that celebrated disability and diversity. 'Cain's Homecoming' is the first of his poems to see publication.

Ian Duhig has written six books of poetry, most recently *Pandorama* (Picador, 2010). He has won the Forward Best Poem Prize, the National Poetry Competition twice and been shortlisted for the T.S. Eliot Prize three times.

Antony Dunn has published three collections, *Pilots and Navigators* (Oxford University Press, 1998), *Flying Fish* (Carcanet Oxford Poets, 2002) and *Bugs* (Carcanet Oxford Poets, 2009). He lives in Leeds. www.antonydunn.org

Mike Harwood has had two plays produced by the Colchester Theatre Group, appeared in a 'Poetry in Performance' event at the Essex Book Festival and read at the launch of *Chimera Five* magazine at Shakespeare & Co bookshop in Paris. His poems were published in the anthology *Genius Floored* (2009) and he has published his first collection *Words Count* (2007). He teaches Creative Writing at the University of Essex and is a founder member of *poetry*wivenhoe.

Tobias Hill is a poet, essayist, writer of short stories and novelist. His fourth novel, *The Hidden*, was published in 2009 and his most recent collection of poems is *Nocturne in Chrome & Sunset Yellow* (2006).

Pam Job has been writing poetry for the last four years and in 2010 won the Fakenham Poetry Competition. She is on the team which organises *poetry*wivenhoe, see www.poetrywivenhoe.org. Currently, she is involved in an Anglo-French poetry project based around the new Wilfred Owen Memorial near Ors in northern France.

Angela Livingstone taught literature (mainly Russian) at Essex University for thirty-one years. She is now retired but going on writing about, and translating, Russian prose and, especially, poetry. She published a lot of translations of poetry by Boris Pasternak and Marina Tsvetaeva, and so far she is most pleased with Tsvetaeva, *The Ratcatcher, A Lyrical Satire* (Angel Press, 1999).

Hilary Llewellyn-Williams lives in Monmouthshire. She is a poet with four published collections from Seren Books, the latest of which is *Greenland* (2003). Her poems have appeared in numerous anthologies, and she gives regular readings of her work. She has been a visiting writer at the University of Essex. Until recently she taught creative writing for the Open University, and she now works as a counsellor/psychotherapist. Her writing has a strongly mythic and spiritual focus. *Hinds' Feet* is a new unpublished poem written as a contribution to this anthology.

Adrian May writes poems, songs and essays, and teaches writing at Essex University. His poems are published by Wivenbooks: *An Essex Attitude* (2009) and *Ballads of Bohemian Essex* (forthcoming). He has also written *Myth and Creative Writing* (Longmans, 2011). Adrian May is a member of the Ukulele Society of Great Britain.

Katrina Naomi's first full collection *The Girl with the Cactus Handshake* (Templar Poetry) was shortlisted for the 2010 London New Poetry Award. Her first pamphlet *Lunch at the Elephant & Castle* won the 2008 Templar Poetry Competition. Katrina's most recent publication is a short collection *Charlotte Bronte's Corset* (Bronte Society), following a residency at the Bronte Parsonage Museum. She is originally from Margate and lives in south London. www.katrinanaomi.co.uk

'Reminiscent of e.e. cummings at his best', **Mario Petrucci**'s work is 'vivid, generous and life-affirming' (*Envoi*). His most recent poems, inspired by Black Mountain and hailed as 'modernist marvels' (*Poetry Book Society*), embrace contemporary issues of searing social and personal relevance via a distinctive combination of innovation and humanity. Through groundbreaking residencies, poetry films and a remarkable output of ecopoetry, his scientific sensibility has illuminated the linguistic as well as emotive resonances of love and loss in the public and private domains. Whether exploring the tragedies of Chernobyl (*Heavy Water*, 2004) or immersing himself in heartfelt invention (*i tulips*, 2010), Petrucci aspires to 'Poetry on a geological scale' (*Verse*).

Clare Pollard has published four collections of poetry, the most recent of which is *Changeling* (Bloodaxe, 2011). Her play *The Weather*, premiered at the Royal Court Theatre and her documentary for radio, 'My Male Muse', was a Radio 4 Pick of the Year. She recently co-edited the Bloodaxe anthology *Voice Recognition: 21 poets for the 21st Century* and is on the board of *Magma* poetry magazine.

Katrina Porteous lives on the Northumberland coast. She has written many poems for radio, including 'Dunstanburgh' (Smokestack Books 2004), 'The Refuge Box' and 'An Ill Wind'. Her poetry collections include *The Lost Music* (Bloodaxe, 1996) and, from Jardine Press, *Longshore Drift* and *The Blue Lonnen*.

Anne Ryland lives in Berwick-upon-Tweed, where she tutors adults and runs writing workshops for community groups. Her first collection, *Autumnologist* (Arrowhead Press), was shortlisted for the Forward Prize for Best First Collection in 2006, and her second collection, *The Unmothering Class*, is due to be published later this year, also by Arrowhead Press.

Penelope Shuttle's ninth collection, *Sandgrain and Hourglass*, appeared in October 2010, from Bloodaxe Books, and was a Recommendation of The Poetry Book

Society. She lives in Cornwall and is the widow of the poet Peter Redgrove.

Pauline Stainer has published seven collections of poetry with Bloodaxe. Her last collection was Crossing the Snowline (2008). In 2009 she was given a Cholmondeley award for poetry by the Society of Authors. She now lives in Suffolk, after moving from the Orkney island of Rousay.

In her literary work, **Joan (Norlev) Taylor** has written a novel, *Conversations with Mr. Prain* (Melville House, 2006/2011) and a historical travel narrative, *The Englishman, the Moor and the Holy City* (Tempus/History Press, 2006), co-edited a poetry collection, *poetrywivenhoe* (Wivenbooks, 2008), and annotated the memoir of a Danish poet and teacher, Cecilie Hertz (Edwin Mellen, 2009). She has also published poems in various places in her homeland of New Zealand and the UK.

Philip Terry is Director of Creative Writing at the University of Essex. His books include *Ovid Metamorphosed* (Chatto and Windus, 2000), *Oulipoems* (Ahadada, 2006) and *Shakespeare's Sonnets* (Carcanet, 2010). He is the translator of Raymond Queneau's *Elementary Morality* (Carcanet, 2007).

Robert Vas Dias, an Anglo-American born and now resident in London, has published nine collections in the UK and USA, the latest of which is *Still · Life and Other Poems of Art and Artifice* (Shearsman, 2010). *Leaping Down to Earth* appeared in 2008, with images by the British artists Stephen Chambers and Tom Hammick; his long poem *The Lascaux Variations*, with images by John Wright, was published in 2009. His poetry and criticism has appeared in about 100 magazines, journals, and anthologies in both countries.

A festschrift, *Entailing Happiness*, with contributions by 35 poets and writers, appeared this year. He is poetry editor of the online cultural magazine *London Grip* (www.londongrip.com) and a core tutor with the Poetry School, London. His website is at www.robertvasdias.com.

Christine Webb's collection *After Babel*, published by Peterloo Poets in 2004, contains a number of re-workings of Biblical material; these include an iconoclastic sequence 'Gospel Truths', from which her three poems in the present anthology are taken. She won the Poetry London competition in 2007, and in 2009 completed a Creative Writing MA at Royal Holloway, working with Andrew Motion and Jo Shapcott. She is a contributor to the Grey Hen Press anthologies *A Twist of Malice* and *Cracking On*; her new collection *Catching Your Breath*, published this summer by Cinnamon, celebrates life with her partner, who died in 2006.

James Knox Whittet was born and brought up in the Hebridean island of Islay where his father was head gardener at Dunlossit Castle. His paternal grandmother came from a crofting family in the Isle Of Skye. He was educated at Newbattle Abbey College and Cambridge University. He has edited two island inspired anthologies: *100 Island Poems* and *Writers On Islands* for Iron Press. His collections include *Poems From the Hebrides*. He has received a number of awards for his poetry including the George Crabbe Memorial Award, the Neil Gunn Memorial Award and awards from the Arts Council of England, Highland Arts and from the Society of Authors. He now lives in a small village in Norfolk with his wife, Ann.

Index of Poets

Lightning Source UK Ltd.
Milton Keynes UK
UKOW050559241111

182608UK00001B/4/P